Sam Dale
Alabama Frontiersman

Tom Bailey

Seacoast Publishing
Birmingham, Alabama

Sam Dale: Alabama Frontiersman

Published by Seacoast Publishing, Inc.
1149 Mountain Oaks Drive
Birmingham, Alabama 35226

Library of Congress Card Number: 00-193309

Cover art by Thomas B. Moore

ISBN 1-878561-82-0

To obtain copies of this book, please write or call:
Seacoast Publishing, Inc.
Post Office Box 26492
Birmingham, Alabama 35260
(205) 979-2909

Dedication

To my parents, Jack and Lillian Bailey, for their great gifts of curiosity and adventurous spirit.

About The Series

Alabama Roots is a book series designed to provide reading pleasure for young people, to allow readers to better know the men and women who shaped the State of Alabama, and to fill a much-needed void of quality regional non-fiction for students in middle grades.

For years, teachers and librarians have searched for quality biographies about famous people from Alabama. This series is a response to that search. The series will cover a span of time from pre-statehood through the modern day.

The goal of *Alabama Roots* is to provide biographies that are historically accurate and as interesting as the characters whose lives they explore.

The *Alabama Roots* mark assures readers and educators of consistent quality in research, composition, and presentation.

The historical drawings that appear in this book are by John M'Lenan, and were first published in 1860 in a book entitled *Life and Times of Gen. Sam. Dale, The Mississippi Partisan* by J.F.H. Claiborne.

Contents

Up a Tree

SAM DALE WAS IN TROUBLE—the kind of trouble that gets people killed.

He was high up in a tall tree, clinging to the trunk.

Directly below him were three men. Two of them were already dead. The third was an Indian, standing right below young Sam. That Indian intended to make Sam the third person to die that morning.

This was the Georgia frontier in the late 1700s. It was a dangerous place.

White settlers had streamed into the lands of the Cherokee and Creek. They chopped down the trees to make fields for crops, and for logs to build cabins.

The Indians and the new white settlers got along for a little while. They traded with each other, visited each other and sometimes married each other.

More and more white settlers came, some bringing

slaves, and they built bigger and bigger farms. The Indians began getting upset as the white farmers began taking over so much land.

The fighting began.

On this cool Georgia morning, 11-year-old Sam Dale found himself in the middle of that fight, hiding behind a tree trunk from an Indian who was aiming a rifle right at his head.

Sam never expected to be in this kind of trouble so close to the fort. But he shouldn't have been surprised.

He knew that Indians were all around little Fort Carmichael where he lived with his parents and eight brothers and sisters. He knew that they were angry.

Just three days before, Sam, his father and some other men barely escaped an Indian attack at a field in the woods where they had gone to dig potatoes.

On that day, the settlers saw the attack coming at the last minute.

"Every one for himself!" Sam's father shouted, and the settlers rode hard for the woods in every direction. The Indians had them surrounded and were shooting from everywhere. By a miracle, they all made it back to the fort alive. Two horses were crippled and a few of the men were wounded.

Blood ran down Sam's face. An Indian bullet had nicked his nose and cut the cartilage.

Fort Carmichael wasn't much of a fort. There were just some cabins in a square, with logs around the outside and a blockhouse on the inside. Fields of corn, potatoes and other vegetables were out from the fort and the settlers would ride out each day to work their fields.

It was autumn. The corn crop had been gathered and the corn stalks had been pulled and piled up. It made good food for cows. So, three days after the potato field attack, two slaves were sent from the fort before daylight to move some cows into the cornfield.

Even though it still was dark, Sam and his brother were awake. They were going to sneak out for a coon hunt. Their plan was to find a raccoon in a tree, shake it down, catch it and bring it back to the fort to eat.

Before slipping out of the cabin, Sam pushed an old pistol into his belt. Just in case.

It wasn't long and the two Dale boys had a raccoon treed. It was a tall tree. Sam climbed high up to shake out the raccoon, while his brother waited on the ground for it to fall.

Suddenly, gunfire exploded in the woods.

Sam's brother dashed for the fort.

At the same time, one of the two slaves who had been putting the cows in the cornfield came staggering along the trail and fell.

The other slave came running up the trail, the long tails of his coat flapping behind him. Three Indians were right behind.

Creeks!

Their bodies were painted for battle.

The trail led right by Sam's tree. All of them—the slave and three angry Indians—were coming right toward him.

The Indian closest to the slave grabbed the slave's coattails, but they tore loose in his hands. The Indian lunged again and this time caught the back of the slave's coat. But the whole coat tore loose. When it did, the Indian fell. The Indian scrambled to his feet and started the chase again, but the slave was too far ahead and got back safely to the fort.

The other two Indians saw the body of the slave who had fallen near Sam's tree and stopped to scalp him. They were right under Sam! They just kept standing there. Sam had no way to escape.

He touched the pistol in his belt. He had only one shot. That morning he had loaded the pistol with buckshot—several small lead balls instead of one big one. Maybe, just maybe, if the Indians stood close enough together and if he could get the right angle, he could shoot them both with one shot.

Quiet as a forest shadow, Sam moved into position. He raised the heavy pistol, pulled back the hammer and leaned into the tree trunk to steady his aim.

He squeezed the trigger and the pistol bucked. For a moment, smoke from the blast blinded Sam from what he had done. As the smoke drifted away, he saw that the shot had killed one Indian, and the other was so frightened that he was running into the forest.

The fight was not over, though.

At that very moment, back down the trail came the third Indian who had chased the slave to the fort.

The Indian had heard the shot, and he saw where it came from.

He picked up the rifle that he had dropped while chasing the slave and leveled it at Sam.

"I had often been baffled for hours by a fox squirrel in a tree watching my motions and going round and round, so as to keep the tree between me and him," Sam told friends later. "I played the same game with the Indian."

Sam had no reload for his pistol, so all he could do was circle the tree trunk to keep it between him and the Indian.

"He fired twice and barked the tree close to my ears," Sam said.

By this time, settlers at the fort were racing down the trail. They followed the sound of the shots and when they burst into view, the Indian ran for the safety of the deep woods.

Through it all, the raccoon watched from the tree's high branches.

The Indian gone and Sam's tree surrounded by family and friends, he climbed further up the tree, shook out the raccoon, climbed down and walked safely home.

Living on the Edge

SAM DALE LIVED A LIFETIME of narrow escapes.

He was born and raised under the protection of a cocked gun in places so wild they barely had a name.

He helped carve the first white man's trail across Alabama, led the first settlers in and fought the Indians to help them keep it.

Sam Dale was to Alabama what Daniel Boone was to Kentucky and David Crockett was to Tennessee.

He lived his life on a dangerous, narrow edge where survival was decided by who was the better aim and quicker shot.

Some say Sam Dale was the bravest, smartest and toughest of Alabama's frontiersmen. Others say he was the luckiest.

Decide for yourself. This is his story.

Sam Dale's mother and father were born in

Carlisle, Pennsylvania. It was a village in the south central part of the state, just east of the Appalachian mountains.

They were Scotch-Irish, part of a tough group who had fled their homeland for America. They wanted to get away from religious restrictions and high taxes that the British rulers were demanding.

Their ancestors had faced bloody fights in Ireland and Scotland, so settling on the American frontier was not a hard choice.

In the middle 1700s, many Scotch-Irish and other European immigrants moved south along the Appalachians, deep into the American wilderness. The Dales were part of that group.

They stopped in Rockbridge County, Virginia, in a wide valley. It was there in a one-room cabin that the first of their nine children was born.

They named him Samuel, and called him Sam.

Sam was a toddler when the Dale's pulled up roots and moved again. This time they settled in the southwest tip of Virginia, on a plot of land at the forks of the Clinch River.

It was mountain country. Unexplored. Deep valleys and giant trees made the forest floor dark even during the day. It was a place where men would go to hunt for game in the forest and sometimes just never come back.

Danger was everywhere.

There were bears, mountain lion, wolves.

Hostile Indians.

The Indians wanted the white settlers to go back where they came from.

Sam's family and others who came with them into this unknown land loved the adventure and freedom to live as they pleased. They were willing to take on the dangers.

"It was a wild, precarious life" that was often interrupted by ambush and massacre, Sam said, "but no one of that hardy frontier race was ever known to return to the settlements..."

The Dales joined other frontier families along the Clinch River to build a fort at a place called Glade Hollow. Men and boys planted corn and tended the crops while others scouted around the fields and kept watch. They kept their long rifles ready.

The women and children stayed in the safety of the stockade.

This was the land of the Shawnee, one of America's most warlike Indian nations.

The Shawnee would hide in the forest darkness and ambush any settler who became careless on a hunting expedition. They ambushed farmers tending fields; raided and burned cabins; kidnapped women and children.

They wanted to push the white settlers out of their territory, and they would do anything that they could to make the white people leave.

Even after he had grown up, Sam still had strong memories of the time his father narrowly escaped a Shawnee ambush.

Sam's father left the fort one day and soon came across a group of men from a nearby village who told him that they had seen Indian signs.

The Shawnees hid in a ravine just outside Glade Hollow. Sam's father and the men from the nearby village approached the stockade not knowing that the Indians were hiding only yards away.

"The terrific war-whoop and the crack of twenty rifles were the first they knew of the enemy," Sam said years later.

Sam's father and the others broke for the fort, but two of their group fell dead.

It was not the only attack that Sam's little community suffered.

Days after the ambush, two settler families went out to clearings in the woods to plant corn. The two men went into the woods to hunt. While they were gone Indians took their wives and children.

Less than a year afterward, Sam's father was away from the stockade, leaving Mrs. Dale and the children. Darkness had fallen when Mrs. Dale saw two Shawnee warriors sneaking up on the cabin.

She put out the fire with a bucket of water so the Indians could not see the family by the firelight, and she made the children lie on the floor. She bolted the door and stood there with an ax and rifle. The Indians never attacked.

Days later, even with the threat of Indian ambush hanging over the region, the Dales and others decided to attend a wedding and party at Clinch Mountain, several miles away. A wedding, feast, dancing and visiting with other families was worth the risk of attack.

When they arrived for the wedding they found burned cabins and six dead and scalped settlers. The bride, her mother and three children were missing. Kidnapped!

The bride and her sister escaped from Shawnees hours later, found their way back to the home site just as the dead settlers, including her father, were being buried. The survivors told the young bride that she should go ahead and marry, and she did so, right beside her father's grave.

Some of the men chased after the Shawnees, caught them and recaptured the bride's mother and a child. The Indians had killed one captive.

Before the year was out, more women and children were kidnapped; some were killed; some were scalped and lived to tell about it.

By the winter of 1783, the Dales had had enough.

They heard about a place to the southeast where farming was good and the Indians were willing to live peacefully with the settlers.

It was called Georgia.

From a Boy to a Man

INDIAN TROUBLE DOGGED the Dale family.

They hardly had time to settle into their new home near Greensboro, when the Creeks and Cherokees began raiding settlements across central Georgia.

The Dales were forced to join about 30 other families at nearby Carmichael's Station (a spot about half way between Atlanta and Augusta).

On one dark night, a band of Creeks slipped up to the settlement and set fire to corn shucks that had been piled against the wall of the fort, and to a building where flax was stored.

This also was the place where young Sam and his brother went on their early morning coon hunt, and were nearly killed by the angry Creek warriors who caught Sam in the tree.

Sam outsmarted the Indians that morning by using a trick he learned from a fox squirrel.

That trick and lots of others that Sam learned by watching animals and people of the forest are what kept him alive in the years to come.

As time passed, more and more settlers poured into Georgia, carving up the land, clearing fields, planting crops and pushing the Cherokees northward into the Carolina Mountains and the Creeks into west Georgia and Alabama.

The Indians finally gave up the fight around Carmichael's Station.

November, 1791, was a happy time for the Dale family.

Sam's father felt that it was safe enough for the family to leave the fort and move onto their own farm.

He found just the land he wanted, only three miles from the fort, and made a deal to swap 7,000 pounds of tobacco for the farm.

They built a new home, and cleared fields.

It was the first time in their life that the Dales did not feel that they were living on the edge of life and death.

The happy time did not last long.

All the horses but one got sick and died.

In December, Sam's mother died.

Sam's father, the man who had been fearless in the face of Indian attack and every kind of frontier hardship, could not live with the loss of his beloved wife.

"He never looked up, scarcely ever spoke, after her death," Sam said, "but took to his bed, and never rose from it again." Within a week of Sam's mother's death, his father also lay dead.

Sam Dale was 19 years old, and the leader of eight brothers and sisters, one just a baby. They were orphans.

What was he to do? What could he do?

"Never have I felt so crushed and overpowered by the feeling of helplessness and isolation," said Sam. The children owned no land. The farm was in debt. They had no other family, nor well-to-do friends to help.

The brothers and sisters buried their father next to their mother, went back to the cabin and cried themselves to sleep.

After dark, Sam slipped out of the cabin.

"I went to their graves and prayed," said Sam. "I went to the grave a broken-hearted, almost despairing

boy.

"I came back tearful and sad, but a hopeful and resolute man."

Something special happened to Sam Dale that night as he prayed at his parents' graveside.

At that moment he took on the job of mother and father to his brothers and sisters. He did it with confidence and happiness that no one could understand.

The next morning when the children got up, Sam was there with a smile, a cheerful voice, and a plan.

Every brother and sister old enough to work was given a job based on what he or she could do best.

Some tended house. Some tended the fields.

Some cooked. Some cleaned.

Some kept track of the bills, and made sure they got paid.

In two years' time, the family farm was beginning to show success, but the land still was not paid off.

To the west, in west Georgia and the land that is now Alabama, settlers were being harassed by the Indians. The trouble gave Dale a way to pay off the farm.

The governor of Georgia ordered a troop of soldiers to be organized to protect the frontier. It was a paying job. Dale volunteered.

It was 1793. Sam Dale was 21 years old, and grown to full manhood. He stood "six feet two inches, erect, square-shouldered, rawboned and muscular," wrote a friend who knew him well.

He was noted "particularly for great length and strength of arm."

He could shoot and fight and ride and live for days in the forest with no shelter and little food.

He was just the kind of man the Georgia governor wanted in his militia.

A coonskin cap, bear-skin vest, hunting shirt and pants of homespun and buckskin leggings was Dale's uniform. He carried a pouch of parched corn for food, a blanket behind his saddle for sleeping, a long rifle and hunting knife for battle.

Dale hired an old man to help his brothers and sisters with the farm, and went to Fort Mathews on the Oconee River in central Georgia. Money from his militia pay and an excellent tobacco crop paid half the debt on the farm the first year.

The next year there was more militia pay and another good crop. The Dales paid off the farm. It was a good time for the brothers and sisters. There was food to eat, and money for supplies. The farm finally was their own, and they were without fear that some-

Tom Bailey

one they owed money to might come and take it away.

Even the Creek Indian attacks on the frontier seemed too far away for them to worry.

For all of them except Dale.

Along the Chattahoochee River cabins were being burned, horses and cows stolen.

Dale's company was ordered out of Fort Mathews to quiet things down.

Little did Dale know that he was again about to stare death in the face.

Dale's company tracked a band of the Indians to a village near the river, won a battle there and started back to their fort.

Dale was lead scout and suddenly stumbled on a Creek lodge. Shots were fired. One Indian lay dead and the other jumped into a thick patch of cane, called a canebrake.

Cane is a tall plant that grows in thick patches in low places along rivers in the South. It is the plant that fishing poles are made from, and looks much like bamboo. The tall cane and blade-like leaves are almost impossible to see through.

The Creek warrior was well hidden.

Dale and a militiaman named O'Neal followed the warrior into the cane.

"The cane was very thick, and we wormed along slowly, when the Indian fired," Dale said later. "O'Neal fell dead by my side."

Dale was deep in the cane. He could not see them, but he could hear the rest of the militia troop riding up behind him.

He knew he was in trouble. He knew the troop couldn't see him in the cane. He also knew they would think that the Indians were in the cane.

Dale was right. The militiamen began firing. Bullets were cutting into the cane all around him. He threw himself to the ground and pulled up O'Neal's body as a shield. Still, two of the shots wounded Dale slightly, but his dead comrade's body saved him from being shot to death by his own men.

When the firing finally quieted down, Dale yelled out his position. His shout caused the militiamen to stop shooting at him, but it also let the warrior hiding nearby know exactly where he lay.

The warrior knew that if he could kill Dale, he could escape out the canebrake on the opposite side from where the militia was firing.

"Gliding through the cane like a serpent in an almost horizontal posture, he briskly approached me," Dale said. "I cocked my rifle, and the instant I got sight of his head I pulled the trigger."

The rifle misfired and before Dale could reload the warrior was on him; "his knife at my throat and his left hand twisted in my hair."

A shot rang out. The warrior's blade never moved. Instead the Indian collapsed into Dale's arms, shot through the heart by one of the militia men who saw what was happening just in the nick of time.

Tom Bailey

Opening the Alabama Frontier

DALE SCOUTED FOR THE MILITIA only two years more. By 1796, the frontier had quieted down again and the troop was disbanded.

Dale bought four horses and a wagon and went into the hauling business in Savannah, Georgia during the fall and winter. In the spring he returned to the family farm to help his brothers and sisters plant the fields.

For three years Dale split his time between farming and wagon hauling. He and his family prospered. By 1799 he had saved some money, and had an idea of a way to make even more money.

He bought some goods to trade to the Creeks.

He took his wagon into the Creek territory and traded his goods for cows, pigs, pelts, hides and animal fat. He carried the Indian goods to the coast and sold them.

As he rolled along over the Creek trails from village to village he ran into more and more settlers moving from Georgia and the Carolinas onto Creek and Choctaw lands in east Georgia, Alabama and Mississippi. At that time, Mississippi and Alabama together were known as the Mississippi Territory.

It was obvious to Dale that these settlers needed help finding their way through the frontier. He knew he could help. He also knew it could make his trading business even better.

Dale bought three wagons and went into business escorting families into the frontier. Heading west, his wagons were loaded with settler families and their belongings, plus merchandise to trade to the Indians. On his return trip east to Savannah, he brought back the Indian goods to sell at the coast. He was making money both ways.

He also was learning the trails, the settlers and the Indians of the land that would become Alabama.

It was a place that would change Sam Dale forever.

The Indians Get Ready for War

THE CREEK INDIANS had lived on the land of Georgia and Alabama long before the first Spanish explorers arrived on the coast and marched inland. When the first white men arrived, the Creeks were the strongest Indian group east of the Mississippi River. They actually were a collection of clans that lived in villages along the many rivers and creeks of the region.

They lived in villages of houses, and were known for their social activities. They enjoyed big gatherings to talk and play ball.

When the first white settlers moved into the territory, the Creeks welcomed them. Many Creek women married white men who traded with the Indians. Such relationships were so common that by Sam Dale's day many prominent Creek chiefs were as much white as

Indian.

They were an intelligent people, and quickly grasped the ways of the white man, even though many of them resented those ways.

Creek men were known for their height and muscular strength. They also were known for their cunning way of making others believe one thing and then doing another.

They were fighters, too. Of the 20,000 Creeks in the southeast at that time, more than a fourth were warriors—their skin tattooed with symbols of their status as fighters. The more tattoos one wore, the greater his reputation as a warrior.

The warriors shaved their heads except for a crest of hair at the crown.

In the late 1700s, the Creek's half-blood chief Alexander McGillivray was a crafty leader and a tough bargainer with the Americans, British and Spanish. All three were trying to win the friendship of the Creeks in their struggle either to capture or hold onto the frontier lands.

McGillivray kept them all guessing, which is what he intended to do.

But McGillivray died in 1793 and Colonel Benjamin Hawkins, the United States agent to the Creek nation, took over leadership of the Creeks.

Colonel Hawkins was kind to the Creeks, and taught them to farm and raise animals. Many warriors hated the white man ways, however.

They also hated a deal that some of their chiefs had made with the white leaders in Washington City.

The chiefs who went to Washington had been talked into allowing the Americans to cut a path through the Indian nation from the Chattahoochee River in Georgia to the Alabama River—a path across almost the whole width of Alabama.

It may have started as a path, but it soon turned into a big road full of settlers who were fanning out along the road, clearing the Indian land and building farms.

Many of the Creeks hated what the path across Alabama had become and what it had done to their homeland.

Warriors grumbled that it was time to push back the white settlers and take back their lands. They heard rumors that Indians in the north were plotting war against the whites, and wanted the Creeks to join them in a great war to take back America.

October was the time of the annual great Creek gathering at Took-a-batcha, the ancient town on the Tallapoosa River in east Alabama. (Near present-day

Tallassee, approximately half way between Montgomery and Auburn.)

Rumors flew that the great Shawnee chief Tecumseh was coming from the north to attend the meeting, and to lead the fight against the whites.

Excitement caused by the rumors brought more than 5,000 to Took-a-batcha, including many Cherokees and Choctaws.

The government agent, Colonel Hawkins was there and so was Hawkins' good friend, Sam Dale.

Colonel Hawkins wasn't upset by the war talk. At worst, he said, the Indians would fight some among themselves.

Dale wasn't so sure it would be that simple.

One thing everyone was sure of happened the day after the Creek council met.

Tecumseh came.

He marched into the center of the town square with 24 Shawnee warriors, and they stood there as still and tall as statues.

"They were dressed in tanned buckskin hunting-shirt and leggins, fitting closely, so as to exhibit their muscular development," said Dale, "and they wore a profusion of silver ornaments; their faces were painted red and black."

Each Shawnee warrior carried a rifle, tomahawk and war club.

"They were the most athletic body of men I ever saw," said Dale.

The group stood in stone silence facing the council house. The many Creeks who were there for the council meeting stared in silence.

Finally, the Creek chief known as Big Warrior walked slowly to Tecumseh and handed him his pipe.

When the pipe had been passed to each Shawnee warrior and back to Big Warrior, the Creek chief pointed to a cabin that had been furnished earlier with skins and food. Tecumseh and his warriors marched into the cabin without ever saying a word.

Each night Tecumseh and the Shawnee warriors danced in front of the cabin as the Creek's gathered around to watch; but no one spoke.

Each morning Tecumseh sent out a messenger to announce that he would deliver his talk. Later each day he sent the messenger back saying that the talk was being put off until the next day.

Colonel Hawkins got tired of the delays and began packing to leave. Dale urged him to say. "I told him the Shawnees intended mischief; that I noted much irritation and excitement among the Creeks, and he would do well to remain."

"Sam, you are getting womanly and cowardly," Hawkins joked as he continued to pack.

Dale packed too and rode out of camp with Colonel Hawkins. "There's danger ahead," Dale warned the colonel as they rode along. "With your permission, since I've got some merchandise in the area, I want to watch them a while longer."

They rode about 12 miles from Took-a-batcha to a place called Big Spring. Dale talked the colonel into staying at the spring for a couple of days. During that time, Dale returned to Took-a-batcha to keep an eye on things.

He met an old and dear friend near the council ground, Bill Milfort, and stayed close to him during the next several days. Milfort was a half-blood, nearly white in color and quite handsome.

Dale once nursed Bill through a serious illness. The two were close.

While Dale remained on the outskirts of the town, Milfort agreed to keep an eye on the Shawnees and let Dale know when Tecumseh was about to speak.

The very next day, at noon exactly, Milfort gave Dale the word. Tecumseh was ready.

Dale and Milfort hurried to the edge of the crowd.

Tecumseh and his warriors marched out of the cabin.

"They were painted black, and entirely naked except the flap about their loins," Dale said. "Every weapon but the war-club had been laid aside.

Each Shawnee wore an angry face.

"Tecumseh led, the warriors followed, one in the footsteps of the other," Dale said.

They marched about the square, dropping tobacco here and there. It was a mysterious ceremony, even to the Creeks.

After a time Tecumseh began to speak, quietly and slowly at first. Then louder and angrier, challenging the Creeks—the tribe of Tecumseh's mother—to join him and throw the white man out of America.

The speech was so powerful that Dale was able to recite it, almost word for word, years later. He said Tecumseh told the Creeks to burn out the whites, "destroy their stock! Slay their wives and children! The red man owns the country, and the pale faces must never enjoy it.

"War now! War forever!"

The Creeks shook their tomahawks, and Dale knew that bad times were coming.

It was nearly midnight when Dale left the council ground for Big Spring to tell Colonel Hawkins what he had seen and heard.

"It's going to be trouble," Dale told him. "Bad trouble."

Colonel Hawkins didn't think so. "It's nothing serious, Sam," he said. "It's just a few fanatics carrying on. None of them have any influence. Most of them like the life they have. They want peace.

Colonel Benjamin Hawkins

"Oh, they might fight a little among themselves," he went on. "But the chiefs will get everything settled down soon enough.

"Believe me," Colonel Hawkins said, "I've worked with these people. I've taught them how to farm and raise livestock. They wouldn't turn their backs on everything I've done.

"Sam, there's no danger here."

"Colonel, with all respect, I believe you're overestimating your influence with the Creeks," said Dale, as the two rode together away from Big Spring.

Dale is Wounded at Burnt Corn

WHITE SETTLERS POURED DOWN the federal road, all across the southern half of Alabama, eastward into Mississippi and southward to Mobile.

They were so hungry for new land and a new start, even the danger of hostile Creeks did not hold them back.

Dale continued guiding them into the territory.

By early summer, 1813, Dale's guide trips found danger on every trail. More than once only good luck allowed him to deliver his settlers to their new homes unharmed.

War was coming soon. Dale had to know when.

He went to see Sam Manac, a friendly half-breed who lived on Catoma Creek. Manac usually knew what was going on.

Just days earlier, Manac had run into an Indian named High-Head Jim, who was on his way to

High-Head Jim

Pensacola to buy bullets and gun powder.

"High-Head Jim asked me what I meant to do, whether I was with his warriors or whether I was on the side of the whites," Manac said. "I was afraid he would have killed me if I said I was on the white man's side, so I told him 'I will sell my property and join you.'"

"So what happened then?" Dale prodded.

Manac said that High-Head Jim was carrying a letter from a British general that would convince the Spanish governor in Pensacola to give the Creeks everything they needed for war.

"After that, High-Head Jim said, the Indians on the Coosa, Tallapoosa, and Black Warrior would attack the settlements in the forks of Tombigbee and Alabama (rivers); that the Cherokees would attack the Tennesseans, the Seminoles the Georgians, and the Choctaws the settlements on the Mississippi."

That was terrible, but what Manac said next worried Sam the most.

"On their way back from Pensacola," Manac said, "they plan to destroy the Tensaw settlements."

The Tensaw is a dark, slow river, its banks choked with Cypress knees. It is one of dozens of streams joining the Alabama and Tombigbee Rivers north of Mobile to form the wide, wild delta.

On the west side of the delta, the ground rises up slow and flat out of the brown water. It is low and marshy, and floods easily.

On the east side, the ground rises quickly, sometimes so quickly that there are bluffs along the river. This is the land of the Tensaw settlements—little villages dotting the eastern high-ground along the riverbanks.

Settlers had hacked fields out of the Cypress, pine and oak forests, and used the logs to build crude cabins and, in some cases, little forts for protection.

This was the edge of civilization. Tough frontiers-men, their wives and children—fighting the forest, hunger, wild animals, the damp cold of winter and the mosquito fevers of hot wet summers.

And, now, they were about to be fighting the Creeks too.

If High-Head Jim made it to the Tensaw settle-ments with guns and ammunition, it would be a slaughter.

Manac's statement was written down, and Dale sent it to Colonel James Caller, commander of a nearby militia regiment.

Dale went to Point Jackson (near the present day town of Jackson) on the Tombigbee River. The settlers there were busy building a stockade to protect them-selves. They called it Fort Madison.

Sam talked 50 settlers into joining him to cut off the Indians who had gone to Pensacola for ammuni-tion before they could return to the white settlements.

He and his settler volunteers joined Colonel Caller and 130 militiamen. They marched out together in search of the war party.

The Wolf-path was a well-worn Indian trail, and Dale suspected that somewhere along its route he would find High-Head Jim and a fellow warrior, Peter McQueen.

They searched in a wide circle, but found no sign of the warriors.

Dale took the lead scout position as the soldiers worked their way along the low ridges to the southeast. When they reached Burnt Corn Creek, Dale knew the Creeks had to be close.

Dale told Caller that he knew the Creek ways well, and wanted to ride ahead of the others and scout the area.

Caller didn't want to take the chance of Dale getting ambushed so he told 15 other men to go ahead with him.

Dale moved slowly through the pines, stepping lightly and blending with the shadows.

One of Caller's officers grew impatient with the slow-moving Dale, spurred his horse and went galloping past.

Dale was furious.

"Halt, sir," Dale shouted. "Fall back, or I will blow you through. On this scout no man goes ahead of me."

The officer may have been tired of Dale's slow pace, but he knew that Dale meant business. He fell back into line.

Not far away, the Indian war party had stopped to eat. Some sat around cookfires near the riverbank, while their horses grazed in high grass at the edge of a swamp.

Dale worked his way along the trail through pine trees on high ground near where Burnt Corn Creek joins the Escambia River. He could smell smoke from cooking fires.

Creeping to the crest of the hill, Dale looked down toward the stream.

The Creeks had no idea that Dale had discovered them.

The Creek Indian War was about to begin.

Dale motioned for his men to remain out of sight, and sent a messenger back to the other soldiers.

They rode up quickly and decided to attack the Indians at once.

The militiamen were new and had little military training; the volunteers had none. Most knew how to shoot, but hardly any knew how to fight a battle.

They charged down the hill toward the Indians, shouting and shooting.

The startled warriors leaped up and fled into the canebrake swamp along the river, and disappeared behind its thick green curtain. Dale and a few others chased the warriors into the cane, but most of the soldiers stopped to round up the Indians' pack horses laden with gunpowder and ammunition.

In the safety of the swamp the Indians were trying to decide what to do. They were outnumbered three to one and, worse, an Indian later said, they only had 13 rifles.

How could they ever win a fight against so many soldiers and so many guns?

They had to get the pack horses, the gun powder and ammunition back.

There was no choice but to fight. Better to fight and die than to return home defeated and without the ammunition they needed for the war.

So they devised a plan.

They stripped off their shirts, and painted themselves for battle.

The best warriors took the few rifles and primed them for the counter-attack.

The others, unarmed, slipped as close to the edge of the canebrake as they dared.

They had a plan that just might scare the soldiers away.

On the hillside above the swamp, soldiers gath-

ered up the Indians' pack horses with their loads of
gun power and ammunition. At that moment, the
soldiers thought that they already had won. And, by
capturing the Indians' ammunition, had stopped the
war before it ever started.

They were wrong.

From behind the cane the empty-handed warriors
let out a great war-whoop, screaming and shouting.
The warriors with rifles, still invisible behind the cane,
fired with deadly aim at the nearest soldiers.

On the open high ground the soldiers were easy
targets among the pine trees.

Dale and several others shot back.

"Early in the engagement, I shot a very stout
warrior, and while reloading my piece I received a ball
in my left side, which ranged round the ribs, and
lodged against my backbone," Dale later told friends.
"I vomited a good deal of blood, and felt easier, and
one of my men reloaded my rifle for me."

Behind Dale, further up the hill, panicked soldiers
ran in every direction. Some came down the hill to
fight. Some ran away in fright. Some didn't know what
to do.

Someone shouted *retreat*, and almost the whole
troop panicked. Soldiers scattered everywhere. One of
the first to flee was the officer who earlier tried to

show up Dale by riding out ahead of him.

Dale lay wounded and looked up as the officer dashed by.

"I hailed him as he passed," Dale said, "and would have shot him if I could have raised my arm."

Dale pulled himself to his feet, found a stray pony and began to ride away when he saw a group of warriors chasing his friend, a man named Ballard, and another man named Lenoir.

In an instant, Dale "resolved to save him or perish.

"I dashed back, followed by a bold fellow named Glass, whose brother had been killed by my side at the moment I was shot."

Lenior was running fast, but Ballard was slower because he was wounded.

"You save Lenoir," Dale shouted to Glass. "I'll get Ballard."

Dale was too late. From 50 yards away he watched as Ballard stopped and shot the nearest warrior, only to be killed by the others before he could reload.

Glass and Lenoir reached Dale and watched in horror as the Indians scalped Ballard.

It was more than the three could stand.

Glass took Lenoir's gun, ran back toward the warriors and shot the one who had just scalped Ballard.

It was all that they could do. They had no time to reload, and the other soldiers already had run away.

Dale, Lenoir and Glass rode from the battlefield to safety.

Many of the militiamen and volunteers wandered lost and scared for days through the tangled river bottom swamps of south Alabama. Some nearly starved, and some nearly went crazy from fear, before finding their way back to the settlements.

At about the same time, Brigadier General Ferdinand L. Claiborne was marching more soldiers to Alabama from Baton Rouge, Louisiana. When Claiborne reached Fort Stoddard, north of Mobile, on July 30, there still was no word of the fate of Colonel Caller.

The general sent out search parties in every direction, and by the middle of August most of the defeated Burnt Corn soldiers had been found.

When they got back, some people made fun of them for losing the battle. Others sneered. The soldiers were so ashamed of what happened, some of them pretended that they had not even been there.

When the Creeks got back to their villages, they were heroes. They felt strong and brave. Their little band with just a few rifles and a lot of war whoops had whipped a whole army of white soldiers.

Winning that battle—really, just a little fight—made the Creeks believe even more that they could run the white people out of their territory.

They lost most of their ammunition in the battle, but they went back to Pensacola and got more.

They were confident.

They wanted blood.

Fort Mims Massacre Makes Everyone Afraid

THE BULLET IN HIS BACK pained Dale terribly.

He struggled to get back to Fort Madison where he would be safe and the settlers would take care of him.

Everyone was scared.

Whole settler families threw their belongings together on wagons and fled the territory. Others took boats south to the safety of Mobile.

The braver ones gathered in the little forts that were scattered along the rivers.

Fort Madison was one of those places crowded with nervous settlers. Every day more showed up in search of a safe place to stay.

Every day they expected the Creeks to attack.

Some mean things happened.

A mail rider was killed in the forest, and the mail stolen.

Farms were raided and burned.

Livestock and crops were destroyed.

There was no big attack, though.

Not right then.

Sam Dale was out of his head with pain. For days he suffered so badly he hardly knew what was going on around him.

He didn't realize how bad things were.

General Claiborne wanted to take an army deep into Creek territory. He wanted to burn their villages and put an end to the violence before the Creeks could get organized for a real war.

Major General Thomas Flournoy was the military commander of the whole region. He wasn't sure that chasing after the Creeks was the best idea. He worried that if too many soldiers pulled away from Mobile to chase down the Creeks, another of America's enemies would attack.

The Spanish already controlled Pensacola, less than a hundred miles to the east.

General Flournoy worried that if he let the soldiers leave to fight the Indians, the Spanish would march right into Mobile and take the city. He could not afford to let that happen.

Since he could not get the army he needed to fight the Creeks, General Claiborne asked for militia volunteers to join his soldiers. They needed every man they could get to protect the little forts that were scattered along the rivers northward from Mobile.

On Monday, August 30, everything changed for the worse.

The attack that everyone had been waiting for happened.

Fort Mims was a little stockade built on high ground a quarter mile east of the Tensaw River.

General Claiborne had assigned Major Daniel Beasley and 175 soldiers to protect the settler families crowded into the fort.

Beasley did not seem to worry much about Indian attack. He let the settlers wander around the area, and never bothered to close the fort gates, even at night.

On Sunday night, August 29, two men raced into the stockade and said they had seen a huge war party just north of the fort. Beasley didn't believe them and ordered them whipped for lying.

The next morning, Beasley wrote General Claiborne a letter describing improvements he had made to strengthen the fort, and how confident he was that his men were ready for any kind of attack.

After sending the letter off with a courier, Beasley sat down with some other officers at a little table just inside the gate.

They played cards and drank whiskey.

A frantic settler rode up. "The Indians are coming!" he shouted.

Beasley was mad because the man interrupted his card game and told the soldiers to arrest the man. But the man rode off before they could get him.

All morning the soldiers played cards.

The soldier who was supposed to be guarding the gate was watching the card game.

A deep ravine carved into the sandy soil ran toward the east side of the fort. By noon it was filled with warriors.

A drummer began to play the signal that it was time for dinner.

The warriors thought they had been spotted. They thought the drummer was signaling for battle.

They leaped from the ravine and raced toward the fort.

Still the soldiers played cards.

When the gate guard finally looked up, the warriors were less than a hundred yards away.

"Indians!" he shouted.

Some soldiers jumped up to meet the attack.

Beasley raced to close the gate, but it wouldn't budge.

He hadn't bothered to close it for so long, sand had piled up around it and he could not break it loose.

He still was pushing on the gate when the first Indian tomahawked him in the head.

The battle lasted all afternoon.

The warriors set the buildings on fire with flaming arrows. They shot into the fort through portholes that were in all the walls. They fought hand to hand with tomahawks and war clubs. They killed soldiers, men, women and children.

Hundreds died. No one is sure just how many. But certainly it was several hundred.

Thirty-six survived by breaking out the back of the fort and running into the forest. A few were taken prisoner.

Between 100 and 200 warriors died.

It was the next day before a Tory Creek—the name given to the friendly Creeks—reached Fort Madison and told Dale of the massacre.

The news spread like lightning through the fort.

Women wailed and children cried. Even the tough frontiersmen gathered in small groups, talking quietly with worried looks.

Dale and some of the officers tried to calm everyone down.

The fort was strong, they said, and they were ready to defend any attacks.

They posted extra guards and kept close watch.

The attack they expected never came.

Fort Mims was the worst massacre of a settlement east of the Mississippi in the history of the country.

It also was the last.

The Creeks never again launched such a bold attack.

It might not have been the case had Dale and the soldiers not used every trick they could think of to defend themselves.

Brave Sam Dale Protects the Settlers

FORT GLASS WAS A TINY STOCKADE a quarter mile from the larger Fort Madison.

Fifteen pioneer families gathered there to get away from the Indians.

They desperately needed help, and a leader.

Dale still suffered with the Indian bullet near his spine.

No matter the pain, he could not turn down the cries for help from the families at Fort Glass.

Now General Flournoy, who still was responsible for the army in the region, had two problems.

If he did not send reinforcements to the little forts along the rivers north of Mobile, the Creeks might attack them one by one. Every fort might have a massacre!

If he sent reinforcements from Mobile, he still was afraid the Spanish would take over.

He never liked defending all those little forts.

It scattered his soldiers all over the frontier.

News traveled so slow that he never knew what was going on at the forts until it was too late to do anything about it.

Finally the general made his decision. He would bring his troops back to Mobile, St. Stephens and Mount Vernon.

Fort Madison would close.

"Sam, you've got to come with us," the officers urged. "You don't have enough help to hold out if the Indians attack."

Dale didn't want to go.

"If I can get ten men to stand by me," he said, "I'm staying."

Dale went from settler to settler to see who would stay.

The day the soldiers marched out of Fort Madison, Dale marched in with 50 volunteers to protect the families that remained.

Their number was not nearly enough to fight off an attack.

But Dale had enough tricks to keep attackers

away.

On each side of the fort, he dug two holes and set 50-foot poles in them. Each night bundles of burning wood were pulled to the top of each pole by a chain.

The bright light from the fires "was brilliant," said Dale. It was so bright that a sneak Indian attack was impossible.

Roofs of the buildings inside the fort were plastered with mud to keep them from being set on fire by flaming arrows.

Each day Dale made sure that everyone at the fort revealed themselves with weapons. "We displayed ourselves in arms frequently," he said, "the women wearing hats and the garments of their husbands, to impress upon the spies that we knew were lurking around an exaggerated notion of our strength."

The forest was too dangerous for hunting. Whenever hogs or cows wandered near the fort to feed, they were shot for food. "I carefully noted the marks and brands," said Dale. Later he paid their owners.

Dale's defense of the fort was brilliant.

General Flournoy still worried about him.

He wrote Dale a letter urging him to close the fort and come to Mount Vernon, just north of Mobile, where many soldiers were quartered.

The dangers were too great on the frontier, and Dale still was not at full strength.

"Many women and children are under my charge," Dale wrote back. "I have sworn to defend them.

"I have a gallant set of boys," he continued. "If you hear of the fall of Fort Madison, you will find a pile of yellow hides to tan, if you can get your regulars to come and skin them!"

Dale stayed put.

Big Sam and the Great Canoe Fight

SUMMER FADED TO FALL.

Creek skirmishes flared up all across Alabama.

No attacks were on Fort Madison.

In early November General Claiborne sent two of his scouts, Tandy Walker and Jack Evans, to Fort Madison to ask Dale for help. The general wanted Dale to send two of his best woodsmen with Walker and Evans on a mission.

Their assignment was to find out what the Creeks were doing along the Wolf-path.

Dale chose Bill Spikes and George Foster for the job.

Little did anyone know that what was about to happen would make Dale an American legend.

The scouting trip was like many others. Keep quiet. Stay out of sight. Listen closely. Bring back news of what was heard and seen.

They were on the way back to Fort Madison when trouble began.

The four camped at Moore's Ferry on the Alabama River.

Walker and Evans dozed on the riverbank. Dale's men, Spikes and Foster, rested in a canebrake, out of sight.

A canoe drifted silently toward the exposed Walker and Evans.

In the canoe with his warriors was William Weatherford. Some called him Red Eagle, the chief who led the Fort Mims massacre!

By now Walker and Evans were awake. They knew instantly they were in trouble.

The warriors fired from the canoe.

Evans fell dead.

Walker was wounded, but scrambled away and was pulled to safety by Spikes and Foster.

The three hurried to Fort Madison and told Dale of their encounter with Weatherford, and the fate of Evans.

Dale sent out scouts to find out what Weatherford was doing in the area. Did he have a raiding party? How many warriors were there? Where were they going?

The scouts brought news of 80 to 100 warriors camped on the east side of the Alabama River.

Dale would not wait for an attack.

"I took sixty men, intending to bury Jack Evans, and, if practicable, attack the enemy," Dale said.

Fort Madison was almost due north of the Mobile River Delta, between the Tombigbee and Alabama Rivers. It was west of a place on the Alabama River called Weatherford's Bluff.

That morning Dale did not march east to the river.

Instead, he marched southeast and when he reached the river he crossed in canoes to the eastern bank.

That night the men slept in a canebrake.

"At daylight I manned each canoe with five picked men," said Dale, "and directed them to move cautiously up the river, while the rest of us followed the trail which ran along the bank."

Dale put Jerry Austill in charge of the canoes. Austill was a tall, strong 19-year-old, and very tough.

They worked their way north, up river. Dale and 50 men following the shore trail; Austill and nine others in the canoes.

Up ahead, paddling up river, a canoe suddenly came into view.

Dale motioned for Austill to hide the canoes under the bluff that towered over the Alabama River's eastern bank. Dale and his men charged ahead along the trail, trying to catch up to the canoe.

The chase was on.

The Indians in the canoe spotted Austill and paddled faster.

Dale and George Foster raced ahead of the others to catch up. The bluff gave way to swampy ground and the trail turned away from the river to go around.

The trail made a sharp turn and Dale and Foster ran headlong into a group of five warriors.

The lead warrior threw up his rifle to fire.

Dale was quicker.

He fired first and the Indian leader fell on the trail.

Right behind Dale, Foster fired and the warriors fled into the canebrake that lay between the path and the river.

Dale looked down at the tall handsome young warrior he had just shot. It was a man he knew well, a man he once knew as his best friend.

Bill Milfort.

The Bill Milfort he once nursed to health from a serious illness. The Bill Milfort he stayed with at Took-a-batcha and who brought him word when Tecumseh was about to speak.

Weatherford had talked Milfort into joining the war.

It was Milfort's first war path.

And his last.

Dale knelt by his old friend, and looked for a long moment into Milfort's face. A tear rolled down Dale's cheek and dropped.

Dale split his men, putting 30 on the east bank of the river, and going with 20 to the west bank. Austill still had the others manning the canoes.

They worked their way to a spot known as Randon's Landing where they found fires burning and meat drying on scaffolds.

Indians had to be nearby, but none were seen just then.

It was late morning when Dale saw a huge canoe clear a bend just up river.

The boat was a stout 30 feet long, carved from a single Cypress trunk, four feet deep and three feet wide. Inside were eleven Creek warriors. They were painted bright colors, and naked except for loin clothes. The one in front wore a panther skin around his head and down his back.

The canoe turned toward a canebrake, not far

from where Dale was watching.

"I called to my men to follow, and dashed for the canebrake with all my might," Dale said. "Only seven of my men kept up with me."

Just as the Indians reached shore, Dale and his men fired.

Two Indians jumped into the water. Dale shot one and a man named Jim Smith shot the other.

Six Indians lay down in the canoe to keep from being shot. Three others leaped into the water, keeping to the side of the canoe away from Dale and his men. They swam toward deep water, away from the white men, being careful to keep the canoe between them and the deadly guns.

"They are spoiling us!" one Indian yelled from the canoe. Dale knew he was calling out to Weatherford for help.

Dale scanned the riverbanks and into the forest. He could not see Weatherford, but he knew that the chief was close.

Every time the warrior rose up to call out, Dale and his men fired. None of them could hit him.

The warrior raised up in the canoe and taunted the men on the riverbank. "Why don't you shoot?" he mocked them, raising up in the canoe until his chest was exposed. He let out war whoop after war whoop, daring Dale and his men to shoot.

Dale had had enough.

He raised his rifle, took careful aim and fired.

The warrior fell dead.

The canoe began floating downstream in the current, and Dale called out to his men on the opposite bank to get the boats and go after the canoe.

Six of his men leaped into a canoe and paddled for the drifting Indian canoe. Since it was floating with the current with no one paddling, they thought that all the Indians had been shot.

They pulled alongside and the first to look in shouted with shocked surprise, "Live Indians! Back water, boys! Back water!"

He was shouting for the paddlers to back their canoe away from the Indian canoe. In the bottom of the Indian canoe lay the warriors, not dead at all, but simply laying low to keep from being shot.

They were mad. They had tomahawks and guns.

Dale decided to go after the canoe himself.

These Creeks were part of a war party.

They were part of Weatherford's war party, the same ones who only days before had killed General Claiborne's scout Jack Evans.

They had laughed at Dale's men, and taunted

them.

Dale's blood was up.

"Bring me a boat!" he shouted to a man named Caesar.

Caesar was on the opposite bank, and was not sure he wanted to get involved. He acted like he didn't hear Dale.

"Bring me a boat or when I get to your side of the river I'll shoot you!" Dale yelled.

Caesar knew that Dale was a man of his word, so he pushed off in a canoe and met Dale a hundred yards down river from the drifting Indian canoe.

Jim Smith and young Jerry Austill, two of Dale's toughest and most trusted men, joined him in the canoe.

"Take us close, Caesar, and we'll give them a broadside," Dale ordered.

Caesar paddled to within 120 feet of the canoe and turned so that all three men could fire at the same time. They raised their rifles and fired at once.

All three rifles misfired.

The warriors knew it would take at least a half minute for the men to reload—more than enough time to reach Dale's canoe.

With or without loaded guns, Dale was ready for the fight.

Paddlers in each canoe pushed their boats toward each other with long, deep strokes.

As they came close together, an Indian rose up and hurled a scalping knife at Dale. It came in low, sliced through the side of the canoe and grazed Dale's leg.

The canoes bumped. "Grab hold, Caesar," Dale snapped. "Grab hold!"

Caesar pulled the two canoes tightly together and Dale leaped up; one foot in his canoe and the other foot in the Indian canoe.

A warrior right in front of Dale fired point-blank at Dale's chest. The powder in the pan flashed, but the charge did not ignite.

The fight began so fast Dale had no time to react.

Before he could move, the Indian turned his rifle around and swung it at Dale like a club.

The butt of the Indian's gun glanced off Dale's rifle, and in that split second, Dale struck back. He crashed his own rifle over the Indian's head.

Dale turned just in time to see another warrior smash a tomahawk into Austill's head. Dale whirled and hit the warrior across the head so hard that the stock broke away from the barrel.

Austill was dazed, but alive. He grabbed the barrel of Dale's gun and began clubbing the other Indians in

the canoe. Dale grabbed the stock and threw it at the nearest warrior.

Caesar was beginning to lose his grip, but before the Indian canoe tore loose, he handed Dale another gun. This one had a bayonet attached.

The boats inched apart.

The smart thing was for Dale to stick with his canoe, and find another way to get at the warriors.

He was too filled with battle.

Dale leaped alone into the Indian canoe.

As Austill, Smith and Caesar drifted hopelessly away, Smith fired one last shot, wounding a warrior who was about to attack Dale.

Now Dale stood without help in the center of the enemy canoe.

Two warriors lay dead at his feet. A third one, just wounded by Smith, lay in the stern with a rifle that he fired over and over at Dale. Every time, it misfired.

Four powerful, angry warriors were in front of him. If they could have attacked Dale all at once they surely would have killed him.

But the canoe was too narrow. The warriors would have to fight Dale one after the other.

The first warrior swung his rifle at Dale's head like a club.

Dale knocked it away with the barrel of his own rifle, then stabbed the warrior with his bayonet.

The second warrior leaped to attack when a shot rang out.

The warrior dropped into the bottom of the canoe.

Dale looked up toward the other canoe and saw the puff of smoke rising from Austill's rifle. He had reloaded just in time!

The third warrior leaped at Dale with raised tomahawk, and he too was slain by the bayonet.

Only one warrior remained.

It was a Creek named Tar-cha-chee.

He knew Dale, and Dale knew Tar-cha-chee too.

Dale had watched him wrestle and play ball during Indian competitions before the war broke out.

Tar-cha-chee was the most famous ball player in his clan.

For a long moment the two stood and stared at each other. Tar-cha-chee stepped back to the end of the canoe, shook himself all over as many Creeks did just before battle, and let out a war-whoop.

"Big Sam," he shouted, "I am a man. I am coming! Come on!"

Tar-cha-chee charged over the dead warriors,

yelling, and driving the butt of his rifle toward Dale's head.

Dale dodged.

The rifle butt caught him in the shoulder and knocked it out of socket.

Tar-cha-chee's momentum carried him past Dale, and as he went by Dale stabbed the warrior in the back with his bayonet and pushed him into the bottom of the canoe.

Dale pulled the bayonet loose and Tar-cha-chee, painfully wounded, tried to get up.

"Tar-cha-chee is a man," he said again as he struggled up. "He is not afraid to die!"

Dale stabbed the warrior.

Through the whole fight came a constant click, click, click.

It was the wounded warrior in the stern still trying to fire his rifle.

It never fired.

Stumbling over warrior bodies that now filled the canoe bottom, Dale made his way to the stern. The wounded warrior stared at Dale with defiance and hate.

"I am a warrior," he said. "I am not afraid to die."

They were the last words he ever spoke.

The river fell silent. Dale could hear his own heavy breath. The battle seemed to have lasted a lifetime. Actually, hardly ten minutes had passed.

Downstream, Caesar, Smith and Austill fought against the swift Alabama River current with a single broken paddle to reach the warrior canoe.

Men on both banks stood in awe at the vicious combat they had just witnessed. It was like Gladiators of old, fighting to the death. All of them—Dale's men and Indian warriors alike—had stood on the banks and watched, helpless.

They had never, ever before seen such a fearless deed.

As the two canoes finally reached shore the men shouted that Weatherford was coming for a fight. Dale's men quickly boarded canoes and crossed to the opposite side of the river, away from Weatherford.

The war chief was bitter, angry and outsmarted.

He had watched helplessly as Dale killed his warriors one by one in the canoe. He was without boats and could not go out into the river to help. Had the canoe drifted closer to his hiding place, Weatherford would have shot Dale, but the canoe never came into firing range.

Those 10 minutes of hand-to-hand combat quickly became known as The Great Canoe Fight. The story was told over and over around Indian fires all across the region.

From fort to fort the story spread of how Dale leaped from the safety of his canoe into the Indian boat. They told of Dale, still weak from the bullet wound he received at the Battle of Burnt Corn, fighting warrior after warrior.

There were those who never had seen Sam Dale, but there were few who had not heard of his name and his deeds.

Bitter Cold and Bitter Battle at The Holy Ground

WHILE GENERAL CLAIBORNE FOUGHT the Creeks in southwest Alabama, a backwoods fighter from Tennessee rounded up a volunteer Army of 2,000 men and marched south..

It was Andrew Jackson.

Times were tough for Jackson.

His army had little food and almost no supplies.

Living and fighting conditions were so harsh that the soldiers tried twice to mutiny and go home.

General Claiborne knew he had to do something to help Jackson. But what?

A meeting was called at Point Jackson on the Tombigbee River to decide what to do.

Some wanted to build a fort at Weatherford's Bluff on the Alabama River. The area was well known for plentiful corn and cattle that could be used to supply Jackson.

Some thought the proposed fort was too near the heart of the hostile Creek homeland, and that there were not enough troops available to keep the Creeks from attacking.

The officers argued back and forth, with neither side able to win an agreement.

Dale was there, but as an uneducated woodsman he felt self conscious in front of the well-dressed and well-spoken officers. He sat alone, near the back of the room.

"Sam, what have you got to say about this?" General Claiborne called out.

The officers looked around. Sam Dale? The hero of the great canoe fight? Scout at the Battle of Burnt Corn? Protector of Fort Madison?

Dale was famous already. They all knew about this brave frontiersman.

But where was he?

They looked all around.

A gaunt, haggard, smoke-tanned man rose.

This pitiful man could not be the great Sam Dale.

He wore a hunting shirt of rusty brown, homespun pants and leggings of dressed buckskin.

A bearskin cap sat on top of his head, and a panther skin belt was cinched at his waist.

Yes, it was Sam Dale. It had to be.

"General," Dale said, "there's so many shining buttons here to dazzle a fellow's eyes, I do not know whether the opinion of a frontier man will be listened to."

Dale reminded them of the women and children he had been protecting at Fort Madison. He made it clear that he intended to continue caring for the settlers on the frontier. The new fort to supply General Jackson was needed, even if he had to build it and defend it himself.

General Claiborne listened to Dale, and talked with him over a drink of grog.

"Gentlemen," General Claiborne told the officers after his talk with Dale, "the point is decided. We must build the fort; at all hazards it must be built. General Jackson is advancing and supplies must be secured for him."

The general then turned back to Dale. "Captain Dale, there's a duty to perform—a difficult and dangerous one. May I ask you to undertake it?"

"General, I will do what you wish, or die for it," Dale replied, "and every fellow I have will do the same for you."

"Thank you, Captain Dale—a thousand thanks," said the general. "You have a noble set of boys. Proceed up the river in canoes, reconnoiter both banks, and secure the march of my troops."

The great Choctaw chief Pushamataha was at the meeting too, and agreed to help Dale.

They picked a spot on a high bluff overlooking the Alabama River. A log wall, two hundred feet square, went up quickly, as did block houses and a battery that could fire on every part of the river.

They loaded the fort with supplies, equipment and food for Jackson's army, much of it coming from fields and herds belonging to the Weatherford family.

They called the stockade Fort Claiborne.

One hundred twenty miles up river was the place the Creeks called Ekon-achaka.

The Holy Ground.

While Weatherford was attacking Fort Mims, the Creek prophet Josiah Francis was busy building this secret and sacred community on a bluff high above the Alabama River in Lowndes County (It is just outside the present day town of White Hall, just north of U.S. 80 between Montgomery and Selma.).

Francis said the Great Spirit picked out the spot

for the town, and made it a sacred place.

Francis marked off magic circles around the border of the town, and told his followers that any white man trying to cross the circles would be swallowed up by the earth.

Swamps surrounded much of the town, and there were no roads in or out. Instead, warriors found their way there by trails through the thick forest and canebrakes.

After the Fort Mims massacre, Weatherford and his warriors returned to the Holy Ground with stories and booty taken in the raid.

It was a place where Creek warriors from all across the state would come for safety.

Holy Ground was the place that General Claiborne had to destroy.

If he could defeat the Creeks there, Creek power in middle and south Alabama would be broken.

Jackson would be free to march on the last Creek strongholds along the Coosa and Tallapoosa Rivers, and the bloody war would be over.

It was not a good time to fight, though.

Winter had set in.

It was a cold and wet December, the coldest anyone could remember.

General Claiborne knew that the war would not wait, and neither could he.

His soldiers couldn't believe that General Claiborne was going to make them fight in such horrible weather.

More than a dozen officers signed a petition asking that the attack be delayed. Their men were in no condition to fight, they told the general. The soldiers were threadbare and hungry. Many did not even have blankets or shoes.

The officers knew Claiborne would listen with care and sympathy to their pleas. Whatever his decision, they said, they were with him.

The general could not wait.

He ordered them to march for the Holy Ground.

Without blankets or tents, coats or food, the men marched.

With them marched Sam Dale.

Their loyalty brought tears to Claiborne's eyes. He shook every man's hand as they passed.

Eighty miles out they built a stockade for the sick, and a place to leave their baggage. The march had been hard, most of it through pathless forest.

December 29, 1813, dawned gray, wet and bitter

cold.

The magic circles around the Holy Ground lay before them—circles that Francis said would swallow them into the earth.

Claiborne's men divided into three columns, with Dale leading one column.

They stepped through the circles and the earth swallowed no one.

Francis' believers panicked, fled to the river and swam to the safety of the north shore. Francis was among them.

Weatherford never believed in the magic circles. He did believe in bullets—his and the white man's. He and his warriors stayed and fought.

The soldiers were too strong.

The Indians retreated closer and closer to the river bluff. The soldiers closed in from three sides.

Just before the troops cut him off, Weatherford rode up to the high bluff. He and his horse looked over into the swirling waters far below, then backed away a distance of about 30 yards.

The attacking soldiers stared in disbelief as Weatherford spurred his horse, Arrow, toward the bluff. Horse and rider leaped high out over the water before separating as they fell.

They swam unharmed to the north shore where

Weatherford stood on the bank facing the white soldiers. He raised his rifle over his head, shouted a war whoop and disappeared into the forest.

Shooting continued into the next day, even though the battle was won much earlier.

Dale knew that this battle was the beginning of the end of the Creek War.

He knew that the Creeks knew it too.

The Creeks knew now that their prophets like Francis had no magic to keep the white man away.

They knew that there were no magic circles.

That there was no more Holy Ground.

That many of their prophets were dead.

"It taught the savages that they were neither inaccessible nor invulnerable," said Dale. "It destroyed their confidence in their prophets, and it proved what volunteers, even without shoes, clothing, blankets, or provisions would do for their country."

The volunteers marched back to Fort Claiborne and, soon afterward, disbanded.

Three months later, on March 27, 1814, a thousand Creek warriors gathered for a last great fight on the Tallapoosa River.

They called the place Tohopeka.

The soldiers from Tennessee fighting for Andrew Jackson called it Horseshoe Bend.

Tom Bailey

Fighting With Andrew Jackson at New Orleans

ONLY A MAN WITH THE LUCK of Sam Dale
would ride into New Orleans just as the first shots of
the battle for that city were being fired.

But that's what happened in the winter of 1815.

The Creek War was over.

Andrew Jackson was sent to New Orleans to
protect the city from the British. It was near the end of
the War of 1812. The British already had burned Washington City, and they wanted to capture New Orleans.

Their idea was to take over the middle of
America, and use New Orleans as their base of opera-
tion. That way they could stop people from moving
west across the Mississippi River, and keep the United
States from growing.

Jackson's job was to keep the British from taking

the city.

Dale was there delivering important mail from the Secretary of War.

Dale happened to be in Georgia at the office of Mr. Hawkins, the Creek Agent, when the packet arrived. It had to get to Jackson in New Orleans fast.

Mr. Hawkins and the general in charge of troops in Georgia urged Dale to take the packet to New Orleans.

No one knew the way better than he did. No one would ride as fast and hard as he would.

The early December night was approaching, but Dale didn't wait. He bought a tough little pony named Paddy and rode all night.

A week later he was on Lake Pontchartrain's north shore and hired a fishing boat to take him across.

Dale left Paddy on the north shore of the lake, and found another horse when he reached the other side.

He galloped into the city, dark and nearly abandoned. He rode to Jackson's headquarters on Royal Street (in the middle of what is known today as the French Quarter.).

Dale didn't have to ask where everyone was. From the plains of Chalmette five miles away he could hear cannon fire.

It wasn't Sam Dale's fight. His job was just to deliver the mail to Jackson.

But fight he did.

Dale rode hard for the battle front.

There he found men just like him. Frontiersmen with their long rifles, hiding behind banks of dirt and mud. There were soldiers too, and people from town whom Jackson has talked into helping defend the city.

It looked like a pitiful band against the well-dressed British soldiers.

Dale got off his horse and found a place in the line that needed help.

The British marched up.

The Americans fired.

Again!

And again!

The British soldiers still standing panicked.

They turned and ran.

Sometime after midnight Dale delivered the mail to General Jackson.

Jackson was astonished that Dale had made the delivery in only seven days. Most riders took 14 days to make the trip.

"Are you broken down from all the riding and the fighting?" Jackson asked.

"No sir," he replied.

"Then you must return to (Georgia) as fast as you have come," Jackson said. There was important news of the victory at New Orleans that must be sent back. In an hour the papers were ready.

"Write an order...to mount Major Dale on the best horse to be had," Jackson told one of his men.

"And what," asked Dale, "is to be done with Paddy?"

"Who...is Paddy, sir?" Jackson wanted to know.

"The pony, general, that I brought from Georgia."

"You don't mean to say, sir that you rode one horse all the way from Georgia in seven and a half days?"

"I mean nothing less, general."

"Then...he won't be able to go back," Jackson replied, figuring that the horse would be exhausted.

"He is like myself, general," said Dale. "Very tough."

With that Dale set off on his return trip to Georgia with General Jackson's reports. At the north shore of Lake Pontchartrain, the tough little Paddy was waiting.

The trip back from New Orleans was another kind of battle.

Dale fought the weather every step of the way.

Heavy rain turned to ice as it hit the cold ground.

Rivers flooded. Dale and Paddy swam the swift and muddy currents.

By the time Dale reached a fort on the Tallapoosa River, his clothes had frozen to his body.

Two guards stopped Dale as he approached the fort, and told him that he would have to report to the main guard station about a half mile away.

"I should be dead before I could get there," Dale

said. "I am freezing. Fire the alarm if you choose, but don't shoot me. You know me and you know my business."

One of the guards ran to tell the general that Dale was coming. The general wasn't angry. Instead, he came out of his tent to greet Dale.

"Light, Major Dale, light," he called out, urging Dale to get off his horse, come in the tent and tell his stories of the Battle of New Orleans.

Dale did just that, as he drank hot coffee and slowly warmed by a fire. The officers crowded into the tent, and others pushed close to the door to hear the stories.

Dale told them, and when he finished other men came in to hear, and he had to tell the stories again. He was still telling the stories when the sun rose the next morning.

Finally, the general ordered Dale to bed, and put a guard at his door to keep him from being disturbed.

Dale told the stories again and again in the days and weeks that followed.

It has been the biggest battle that Dale had ever fought in. It also was his last.

The peace that followed sometimes was no kinder to Dale than the wars.

Dale Goes Broke Helping Settlers

THE WAR OF 1812 WAS OVER. The Creeks were defeated. General Jackson had even thrown the Spanish out of Pensacola.

The frontier lands of Alabama were more peaceful than they ever had been.

Settlers flooded in.

The roads were choked with wagons, laden with men, women, children, all their belongings and stars in their eyes.

They saw land of their own, crops, livestock, a place for a new start. A place to make a home.

As things settled down and communities grew up all along the frontier, Dale opened a store in Monroe County near the Alabama River, and divided his time between running the store and farming.

The territory governor also gave him the jobs of tax assessor, tax collector and census taker. He also was put in charge of swearing in justices of the peace, sheriffs and constables.

Everyone on the frontier knew Sam Dale, and trusted him.

In 1816 they elected him to represent his part of the state at a convention to split the Mississippi Territory into two parts—the western half would be called Mississippi; the eastern half would be called Alabama.

The next year, Dale was a delegate to the first General Assembly of the Alabama Territory.

He represented his people well. He also worried about them.

Many of the new settlers were not so tough as the earlier pioneers.

Many were better at dreaming about the new frontier than they were carving out a farm out of it.

No one knew it better than Dale.

He saw them every day, grinding down the roads in broken down wagons, with not enough tools or supplies or equipment to build a home or plant a crop.

They didn't have the money to hire help, either.

From almost half the state they showed up at Dale's store for help.

Just a little equipment until the first crops come in, they said. Just a little loan until things got better. Just a little bread. Just for the children.

Dale looked into their sunken faces and hollow, frightened eyes.

He could not refuse them.

"I had saved four thousand dollars," he later told a friend. "(It was) the result of long years of toil, public service" and sacrifice.

He took every dollar to Mobile and bought everything he could for the settlers, then bought everything that he could get on credit.

"These supplies I distributed, on twelve months' credit, among thousands of people," he said, "many of them utter strangers to me, and it ended in my ruin."

Dale was flat broke.

Many settlers who promised to pay Dale back never did. A few did, but there was never enough money for Dale to repay all his debts in Mobile.

The settlers loved him still and he loved them, even if they couldn't repay their debts.

Alabama became a state and the settlers sent him to the capital to represent them. They kept sending him back for almost a decade.

Then came more Indian trouble.

It was a different kind of trouble, a kind of trouble that broke Sam Dale's heart.

Big Sam's Saddest Job

IN THE 1820s, THOUSANDS OF INDIANS still called Alabama home, but many of the white settlers wished they could make the Indians go away.

The representatives in Washington wanted the Indians out of the way too.

In 1830 they passed a law called the Indian Removal Act. This new law gave the president the right to move the Indians off their land to property west of the Mississippi River where few people lived.

In less than a year the Secretary of War contacted Colonel George S. Gaines and Sam Dale about the Removal Act.

He wanted the Choctaws moved out of Mississippi and Alabama to new land on the Arkansas and Red Rivers in Oklahoma.

Dale didn't like it.

He remembered how all the Indians of the southeast had fought so bravely for their land; how they lived on the land without owning it; and how they loved the land they called home.

Moving out the Choctaws was especially hard for Dale.

They never fought the white settlers as the Creeks did.

When the Mississippi Legislature passed laws taking their lands, the Choctaws just shrugged and sadly got ready to leave.

Dale felt that the Mississippi government had tricked the Choctaws out of their land, but what could he do?

The government had asked him to help move the Choctaws. He agreed to do it.

"I found the great body of the Choctaws very sad," he said.

They moped around their cabins with long sad faces.

Again and again they visited the graves of dead family members.

Even the strongest warriors had tears in their eyes.

They never got ready to leave. When Claiborne and Dale said it was time to go, they just went.

"Some, who had not yet buried their dead—for it is the custom of the Choctaws to expose the dead on scaffolds for a certain time, during which they spend many hours every day weeping round their remains—absolutely refused to go until the allotted time for these ceremonies had expired.

"We left them in their country," Dale said. They came along later.

"When we camped at night, many of them stole back, in the darkness, twenty, thirty, and even forty miles, to take 'a last fond look' at the graves of their household, soon to be trampled upon by a more enterprising and less sentimental race."

Dale loved the Indians, even the Creeks who did all they could to kill him—shot him, tomahawked him, cut him with a scalping knife.

He loved their courage.

He loved their ability to survive in the forest.

He loved their ways, their games, their cleverness.

He admired their will to fight for their land.

As he led them away to another land, he thought that they were more honest and more honorable than the government he was working for.

As he led them away, there were tears on both sides.

Somewhere along the path they gave it a name.

The Trail of Tears.

Epilogue

Ia-cha-hopa was one of the Choctaws who had to move west. Dale paid him for two sections of land in east Mississippi, just a few miles west of the Alabama line.

A little town sprang up. The people named it Daleville.

The government asked Dale to find the Choctaws who hadn't yet moved west and escort them out.

He was riding out on that mission when his horse fell on a forest trail. Dale landed hard. His shoulder was knocked out of socket—the same shoulder that Tar-Cha-Chee had knocked out of socket years earlier in the Canoe Fight. There were bruises everywhere.

After making his way back home, Dale sent word that he was too badly injured to escort Indians any longer.

Andrew Jackson became president. Dale healed and felt well enough to visit his old friend. They spent time at the capital together, but Washington was not Dale's kind of place.

He didn't care for the dandies and the wheeler dealers he saw there. He didn't like how they talked about people behind their backs, or the kinds of mean and ugly words they used.

He rode back home through Virginia and Georgia, "the scene of my early adventures."

It was a sentimental journey as he rode along, trying to find the places of his boyhood.

"Most of it I had traversed when it was a pathless wild beset with enemies," Dale said. "Now I found villages, towns, cultivated fields...wealth and civilization.

"Some old friends I met with," he added, "many were in the grave.

"I went for the last time, to the place where I had laid my poor father and mother so many years ago. Briers had grown over them, and wild flowers too.

"I wept once more over their honest dust, and for others very dear to me, now in the grave, and saddened and thoughtful, returned to my home."

On one occasion long after all the battles were

over, Dale was asked to be the best man in a wedding. The groom-to-be had been in the Creek War and, after its end, he had wandered into the settlements near Montgomery.

There he fell in love and persuaded a young beauty to marry him. For his best man he called on Dale—the man whose courage and honor and honesty he respected most.

Dale agreed to stand beside this man that he too respected for many of the same virtues.

The groom was William Weatherford, the Creek warrior chief.

In Daleville, the people would not let him rest. Just as the Alabama settlers had sent him to the Legislature to represent them, the people of Mississippi elected him to represent them in that state.

He grew old on the farm.

Friends from the frontier days visited.

Some few Choctaws who had escaped the Trail of Tears camped on his land. They were poor, and without a home.

Dale fed and clothed them, and kept them safe.

On May 24, 1841, in his 70th year, Sam Dale died.

He was buried near Daleville, Lauderdale County, Mississippi.

Samuel Dale

1772 Born in Rockbridge County, Virginia, to Scotch-Irish pioneer parents.

1775 Dale and family moves to the forks of the Clinch River in southwest Virginia mountains.

1783 Dale family moves to Greensboro, Georgia, area to escape Indian strife.

1783 Creek uprising in Georgia. Indians fire on Dale and others, grazing his nose and leaving it scared for the rest of his life. Indians also trap Dale in a tree while he was hunting raccoons. Dale family moves to nearby Carmichael Station for protection.

November, 1791 Dale's father moves the family to a farm three miles from Carmichael Station that he agrees to buy with 7,000 pounds of tobacco.

December, 25, 1791 Dale's mother dies. A week later his father dies, leaving him and his eight brothers and sisters orphaned.

1792-1793 Dale, his brothers and sisters work the

family farm.

1793 Dale volunteers for militia that is being organized to defend against Creek uprising.

1796 Militia disbanded. Dale purchases horses and a wagon and goes into freight hauling business in Savannah, Ga., in winter. Farms in spring.

1799 Settlers begin moving into the Mississippi Territory, which consisted of the land now occupied by Alabama and Mississippi. Dale buys three wagon teams and begins escorting settlers into the newly opened territory.

1803 President Thomas Jefferson orders a highway marked out through the Mississippi Territory. Dale is selected as a guide for the expedition.

1807 Dale engages in trading expeditions among the Cherokees and Creeks.

October, 1811 The Shawnee chief Tecumseh gives speech at Creek council meeting, and urges them to declare war on the whites.

June 18, 1812 The United States declares war upon Great Britain. It becomes known as the War of 1812.

Early summer, 1813 Party of Creeks go to Pensacola to buy gunpowder and ammunition from the Spanish to use in war against white settlers.

July 25, 1813 Colonel James Caller of the Mississippi Militia joins Sam Dale and 50 volunteers to cut off the Creeks on their return from Pensacola.

July 27, 1813 Caller and Dale encounter Creeks near junction of Escambia River and Burnt Corn Creek. Skirmish becomes known as Battle of Burnt Corn, the first engagement of the Creek War. Dale is wounded in the fight.

July 30, 1813 Brigadier General Ferdinand L. Claiborne leads 550 U.S. Army volunteers from Baton Rouge, Louisiana, to Mount Vernon, Alabama, near Fort Madison.

August 30, 1813 A Creek war party attacks Fort Mims on the Tensaw River, killing several hundred men, women and children. Dale recuperates from wound at Fort Madison.

November 12, 1813 In the middle of the Alabama River, Dale fights a band of Creeks in a canoe and almost single-handedly defeats six of them in hand-to-hand combat. It is a story with heroic qualities that spread quickly across the frontier.

November, 17, 1813 Dale and troops of General Claiborne begin erecting fort at Weatherford's bluff on the Alabama River. It is named Fort Claiborne and will be used as a supply base for General Andrew Jackson.

December 13, 1813 Dale marches with column of General Claiborne's soldiers from Fort Claiborne to attack the Holy Ground, sacred Creek village on the Alabama River in Lowndes County.

December 23, 1813 Holy Ground is attacked. Creeks are defeated. Chief William Weatherford leaps from bluff on horseback and escapes.

March 27, 1814 General Andrew Jackson and Tennessee volunteers defeat Creeks at Horseshoe Bend.

August 9, 1814 Chief William Weatherford—also known as Red Eagle—signs treaty with General Jackson, ending the Creek War.

November 1814 Andrew Jackson captures Pensacola from the Spanish.

December 10, 1814 British ships anchor at Ship Island, off the Mississippi coast, in preparation for attack on New Orleans, Louisiana.

January 8, 1815 Dale participates in Battle of New Orleans, after arriving there with military mail for General Jackson.

1816 Dale elected a delegate to convention called to divide Mississippi Territory into Mississippi and Alabama.

1819 Alabama becomes a state.

1819 - 1828 Dale serves several terms in the Alabama Legislature.

1821 State of Alabama confers on Dale the rank of brigadier general in the state militia.

Sam Dale: Alabama Frontiersman

November, 1824 Dale County, in southeast Alabama, named in Dale's honor by the sixth annual session of the Alabama General Assembly at Cahawba. The town of Daleville, in the southwest corner of Dale County, was settled in the 1820s and also was named in Dale's honor.

1830 Congress passes Indian Removal Act.

1832 Dale is appointed to supervise removal of Choctaw Indians to land in the west. Later that year, Dales visits President Andrew Jackson in Washington.

1830s Dale serves in the Mississippi Legislature.

May 24, 1841 Dale dies at his home near Daleville, Mississippi.

About the Author

Tom Bailey grew up in Pinson, Alabama, attended Jacksonville State University and became a reporter for *The Anniston Star*.

Later he went to work for *The Birmingham News* as a writer and editor.

He has written seven books about Gulf of Mexico fishing, diving and tall tales. He also wrote a joke book about Alabama football. Alabama fans didn't think it was funny.

He and his wife, Jan, live with their daughter, Olivia, in Hoover, Alabama. Their son, Drew and his wife Natalie, live in Atlanta, Georgia.

Julia Dale Wilkinson,
   mother of:
Janet Dale Barrow,
   mother of:
Agnes Dale Plant,
   mother of:
Susan Dale Mason Mason.